Books by Kito and Ling Productions

For Adults:
www.loginthesoul.com

Echoes of a Vision of Paradise:
If you cannot Remember, You will return, Volumes 1 - 3

Echoes of a Vision of Paradise:
If you cannot Remember you will Return, Synopsis

Restoring the Heart

The Simulator

For Children:
www.loginthesoul.org

Andy Ant and Beatrice Bee

Beauty Is on the Inside

Bee and Fairy Power (A short novel in which the Beings of Nature use the super-power Virtue of Love to help humans Grow Organically)

How Alexander the Gnome found the Sun

Katie Caterpillar finds Her Song

Return to Paradise (A short novel in which Happy the Bluebird and Bright-Wings the Cardinal use Virtues to bring back Paradise)

The King and the Castle

ECHOES OF A VISION OF
PARADISE

IF YOU CANNOT REMEMBER, YOU WILL RETURN

A SYNOPSIS

FRANK SCOTT AND NISA MONTIE

BALBOA
PRESS

A DIVISION OF HAY HOUSE

Balboa Press books may be ordered through booksellers or by contacting:

Balboa Press
A Division of Hay House
1663 Liberty Drive
Bloomington, IN 47403
www.balboapress.com
1 (877) 407-4847

ISBN: 978-1-5043-4258-2 (sc)
ISBN: 978-1-5043-4259-9 (e)

Library of Congress Control Number: 2015916424

Print information available on the last page.

Balboa Press rev. date: 12/16/2015

CONTENTS

FOREWORD

We are ***entities***, potentials in ***transit and transcendence***, from one to other Worlds of God.

We call ourselves ***Homo sapiens***, humans by agreement.

We are ***Soul-possessing***—the engraved image of the Creator through which He reveals His Beauty. This gives each of us a Soul-based state of Awareness—tenth-dimensionally speaking.

We are ***Spirits***, imperceptible fields of activity, the precursor engine of all that becomes manifested. There are thus, on Earth, four kinds of Spirit-based effects—a fifth-dimensionally-based, unified system of intelligent life, layered, enfolded and embedded into superposed realities that know neither beginning nor end:

1. The mineral domain, based on attraction and repulsion.
2. The plant domain, based on replication—growth and the induction of the mineral's imperceptible activities.

3. The animal domain, based on instinctive intelligence—incorporating through digestion the plant and mineral domains.

4. The human domain—which by digestion incorporates the previous three domains and is endowed with a physiologically-based consciousness.

We are gated in and out, and piped through tunnels of light when moving through realities, in states of pure awareness.

We have a body arranged in stages, joined together in pairs (phase conjugation), and modulated—the imposition of signals (information) upon everything as stand-alone, scalar (continuous) carrier waves, the fabric of creation. This influence (programming) upon us appears in three formats: egoic modulation (self), environmental (inherited and adapted), and Soul-based (from the Creator).

We are **Seekers** of **Knowledge** and ***the Love of God***, once we are connected to the Root (the Soul), responding to the Clarion Call from the Beloved, forming communities of the Called (Christian, Jewish, Islamic, Buddhist, Hindu, Zoroastrian, Baha'i, and others), awaiting to be Chosen, obtain our Missions, and assist in the advance of an Eternal Civilization, having each found, through the journey, his or her eternal companion; we exist to serve God, Lord of all the worlds, eternally.

The Love of God is the Key that opens all these Worlds of God!

This Love coalesces, through each fractional, temporal existential experience (one of many), the Soul-based Awareness, the Spirit, Mind, and Body, into a state of Oneness (the Whole) and Unity throughout, within individuals, and among families, communities, states, nations, and between this and other worlds, in an ever-growing unified system of intelligent life—planetary, galactic, and of universes—addressing the sixth-, seventh-, eighth-, and ninth-dimensional states of understanding, as we open the portal of our Heart and Soul...

The road to coalescing into a state of conscious-awareness is best illustrated through the Writings of the latest Manifestation of God, Baha'u'llah (a title meaning "*the Glory of God*"), particularly two epistles entitled respectively, *The Seven Valleys* and *The Four Valleys*.

We are dealing with stations of understanding in non-linear space and time, omni-dimensionally and multi-directionally presented, in order for us to experience the gradual Reunion with the Beloved.

SECTION 1

CREATION

Everything has a beginning, and it may not be the kind of beginning that can be easily understood in its entirety. This lack of holistic understanding, of course, is part-and-parcel of having a fourth-dimensional instrument, an environment—the mind, time, and energies—dictating and impressing linearly, how we view our abstract world-constructs—points of spatial locations that help identify where we are, and sequentially over time into categories that present experiences in a certain order, as past, present or future. These mental constructs shape our understanding and opinions of our spiritual journeys, each time we go through the tunnel (when we incarnate) and have first-hand knowledge of a temporal, fractional, existential experience that has a beginning and an end. Caught within the time-space continuum, we cannot come to the true understanding of what is going on. Because we, as entities, don't start here on Planet Earth, our beginnings fall outside the definition applicable to how we view, experience, and understand our Selves in time, when time has no known beginning and a known end. This end is the entry point of each projected Self into a particular temporal, fractional, existential experience, in this case, on Earth.

It is at this moment that a shift takes place, moving us from one type of realm into another quite dissimilar and unfamiliar, where we need to acquire a unit, a body, to be able to observe and participate thereafter in the experience of a life that is meant to bring us into the realization of both the journey and its purpose—how to remember and be able to return to that beginning that knows no beginning and experience Reunion with the Beloved—while serving one another.

Understandably, the nature of a process of a layering of realities that is composed of superposed systems of an intelligent and unified structure, and body of creation, does not at first clearly demonstrate the complex nature of its fabric, nor the underlying map that helps define an omni-dimensional and multi-directional system of light pathways— tunnels— built within, that assist the transit and transcendence (piped, and gated in or out) of us as Light Beings. An immense and complex network throughout Creation, this structure supports and is meant to promote, a condition of conscious-awareness—**Self-remembering**—that gives rise to a community unified and coalesced into an expression of Oneness around Principles brought in by the Manifestations of God, the Creator. These Divine Attributes should adorn us throughout the journey of development, beyond the limits of any one of its layers, thus containing characteristics by which something is recognized as being essential to our understanding of the Reality that should emerge each time.

We as entities, ***Light Beings*** (as subject to enlightenment), able to travel upon and across from one place and reality to other places and worlds, discover soon enough, with the aid of Those that Manifest the Source, that there is a narrative far larger and more cohesive than the one we remember or are able to put together independently. When we recognize These Representatives of the Creator, it is a sign that we are ready to respond to the Clarion Call, an invitation that can set in motion our freedom from our ignorance and mismanaged passions, and assist us in ***Remembering*** our connection to the Source, and be able to ***Return*** when chosen—when we make the grade!

Every time we emerge in a Unified System of Intelligent Life, a World of God, we need ***to be consciously-aware*** of the importance to find He Whom God made Manifest, and become ***Seekers of the Truth*** which stops all our delusional constructs from obscuring the ***Path of Remembrance and Return***, mental constructs that stand in opposition, time and again, to God's ***Divine Plan***.

When we accept the Will and Desire of God, become illumined and transformed, and acquire and practice the ***newly-dispensed*** (Revealed) ***Divine Information***, these energies are released.

Set free from a quagmire built from not Knowing and not Loving the Creator, during each attempt to understand and possess this Earthly (or any other temporal and fractional world) reality as part of our overall journey—***we become divinely modulated and guided***.

We are Light Beings precisely because we can experience Enlightenment: divine information that emanates from God, that results in a certain understanding and an up-lifting that brings ***the Realization of the kind of Life*** that serves our ***true purpose and Mission***, bringing to existence first-hand knowledge (the first point of view), which clarifies our fractional and temporal journeys as we go through them, a Whole that helps us transcend each moment.

This ***Divine Modulation*** (Information imposed upon each of us, ***Soul-based***) gives our Selves a greater purpose and significance, assisting us in **Returning** as fully-realized entities in transit towards the ultimate experience—***Reunion with our Beloved***—and as servants of each other always.

There is many a meaning hidden beneath this statement. To be re-united means *to **experience again*** the bliss of being together once more! This coming together—to experience the Reunion with the Beloved—is ***the Purpose of the journey***, and it entails the acquisition of many attributes that uplift and enhance ***our understanding gifted by the Creator***, as well as assists us in obtaining opportunities to be fully aware (***a Soul-based state of being***) and conscious (***a physiologically-based condition***) of His Love. This state of conscious awareness is an on-going process that causes us to unite, in one body and moment, the Soul, Spirit, mind, and body, bringing about the Oneness of it All—the understanding of the true Purpose of the journey, through service and the advance of an eternal civilization—in each of our Missions when called and chosen.

The Creator's Image is within us all, and His revealed Beauty is ever-present.

Here we are, specks of dust in a bowl we hardly comprehend, slowly moving, crawling along from one place to another, barely able to tie our shoes and get along with each other.

The act of being created needs to be experienced to gain a full perspective, one of the many invitations that will adorn your awakening during your journey.

What if you were to go through a process taking you out of the oven of Creation (that is cooking you to perfection), and into the moment ***before*** the launching of your journey into ***I-ness***? What if you were to be gifted by your Creator with an experience of your coming into Being? Certainly, upon returning to this plane of existence, your perspective would be changed.

Marked by an inquisitive interest, you would move away, time and again, from the familiar or customary, making your life, potentially, an extraordinary one.

Created by an act that is found deep within the Immemorial Essence, in a flow of the eternal that knows neither beginning nor end, your essence is brought into existence by God's Knowing and Loving, out of a descriptive nothingness and true poverty, that binds you forevermore to that Source, and for as long as you ***Remember that moment***, you are experiencing an ever-present Return.

This ever-present return can be Known and realized, time and again, through every living being, as well as anything that partakes, and is a part of, His Creation.

This is especially true when coming together with one's eternal companion. Throughout a journey that will take you as long as it needs to take, **one of the musts** that needs to be experienced, and to bear its fruit, is when the two of you meet in an embrace that will know no end.

SECTION 2
AWAKENING

We are all immersed in a ***Sea of Consciousness***, each of us a very small light immersed in an immense state of darkness. We are only aware that we are aware of an unknown all around us that brings a sense of uncertainty. The light represents our consciousness, what we know and perceive from the world around us.

We move about, trapped in this reality built from our desires or the desires of others, and we go through having first-hand knowledge of myriad temporal and fractional existential experiences, as many as needed, immersed in that Sea of Consciousness, pursuing whatever fancy our hearts desire. We go on and on, life after life, each a track of time that knows a beginning and an end—***our immortality*** at work.

You will always have the opportunity to come to or hear from the Representative of the Creator, your way out of a Loop that has no apparent beginning or end in sight—***to reconnect with the Source*** and ***acquire***

an Awareness of it All.

How you will fare is up to those auspicious ___chance___ encounters. You

have heard of the saying, ___many are called and few are chosen___. But

what does it mean? ___Being called___ indicates that God is giving you the

opportunity to get out of your Loop, that the moment has arrived to

change realities—the way you perceive your journey.

Yet, there are no guarantees. You may choose to ignore the call or find

an excuse to keep on pursuing your fractional-temporal dream or dreams.

This may have happened hundreds of times, and that is why you are still

here.

Few are chosen to leave this self-made construct that moves you

through a labyrinth, a complex system of light tunnels you have been

gated in and out of, as you have gone through hundreds or more of these

temporal and fractional existential experiences—***your journey***.

When you have not been chosen to escape your trap, it is because

you have allowed those temporal desires to be a god ruling your higher

Self, bringing about your ego-modulated dreams time and again! Over

many lives, in many worlds, you have chosen to create your own plans

and reality, or to feel sorry for yourself, or to express anger, jealousy, and envy, or to pursue carnal desires versus pure Love—you keep returning, and you have not remembered.

Once in a while, you get a glimpse, a moment of clarity. You may struggle from within for a short while, and then dismiss the whole idea. You think again, ***that you know better, that you can do it by yourself***; that life is there to be taken, and conquered, that everything can be had and possessed—at least in this life. In other temporal and fractional existential experiences that may not have been the case!

So many times and situations precede this one life. So many other worlds and tracks of time—you cannot remember them. You have returned time and again to a ***different world*** to be given another opportunity to surrender to a Reality that you have been running away from, ever since so long ago.

What is of interest is, that you don't really know that you are caught in this loop. More importantly, you cannot ever detect the difference, be consciously aware that there is something else that beckons you to change the way you observe and participate, inviting you to be transformed and transcend your present condition, your conscious state, and become ***aware that you are aware***—not forgetting your Self!

Yet, you are in an ever-present potential state, in transit and transcending, forwards or backwards, progressing or regressing. You are unconscious of this process insofar as the journey. You may, however, have taken a quick look, gotten a chance to observe and look deeper into the life you are pursuing. But that is all. You go on ahead without further thought—the game is afoot, Watson.

You may have had dreams, telling yourself to awaken, to come to realize the futility of your ways. These are moments of clarity, at some particular point in time, whenever they arrive, when things do not seem right.

Despite the **Call**, everything is allowed to go back to the way it was, the script, part of your narrative, the role-playing as a man or a woman, the props and costumes that help you play the role, along with the rituals, culture, and language used to convince yourself and others that you know how to play the game.

We live in communities reflecting our success or failure to walk the talk. We are part of cultures and belief systems, in line with roles and scripts. We have dreams, things we pursue. We have brought in certain abilities accrued over the journey, inherited other tendencies from the unit (the body), and been influenced by an environment that has furnished us with a glut of information hard to keep-up with, *modulations inherent* in our journey, imposed upon on each of us as *stand alone scalar carrier waves*—a fancy term that identifies how we come to this or any other world we partake of, throughout our sojourn in the here-and- now—*the Spirit* in everything.

Nonetheless, what is important to understand is that you are immersed in a *Sea of Awareness*, the universe you are in, of which you are only conscious of, and within the span of a life, the moments you are focused on—some eight seconds at a time. This is a pretty short time if I may point out—the goldfish's attention span is nine seconds.

So how do we stop this merry-go-around journey, the Loop that consistently traps each of us again and again in roles, scripts, costumes, and props? How do we break out of the loop occurring even in cultures within the communities of those that are, or were, *Called*, or within groups with some other inherent interest or practice, within families with traditions and rituals handed down the pipeline, within all the beliefs that are practiced in that world: the politics of appearances, the trance and trap that molds us into something else?

How do we come out of the labyrinth and walk the straight path?

How do we independently find the Manifestation of God for this Day and Age?

For it is the latter quest that is the surest path to awakening once and for all. Every one thousand years, a little more or less each time, the

Creator calls everyone and ***assesses those that He chooses to awaken***, to invite to experience Reality, something totally different—***reunion with the Beloved***.

This is how it begins.

The ***first step*** in the process of ***enlightenment*** is to ***recognize*** the Manifestation of God for the day and age of development and opportunity in which we live. This pre-requisite cannot be avoided and should not be delayed. What do we mean by the word ***Manifestation***? It refers to Someone Who is clearly a channel for the expression of God, the Creator, and can be recognized through the way He speaks, writes, and lives—the Word.

The ***second step*** is to ***surrender*** one's whole Self to the administering influence of God. Let there be nothing left of one's personal self (the projected persona and construct, the ego).

The ***third step*** is ***to enjoy the ride***: God has in store greater and greater levels of blissful experiences as one becomes less and less attached to the things and desires of each world.

The ***fourth step*** is to ***give thanks continually to God***, the Creator of all, for without Him, you would not exist.

These are the four ***main steps to enlightenment***—a way out of the trap and the Loop your journey has become. There are other, smaller steps that are contained within these. These steps will become apparent as you gradually ascend out of the mire of delusion—the erroneous beliefs, mistaken ideas, and mismanaged passions that hold you prisoner.

Do not be tricked by the **Master Game** many pursue, by those who promise to have the answer, that claim to know the way! It is meant to be your own journey. How else can you tell the difference between Truth and falsehood? This is a process of exploration and discovery; when ready, you will know. These are actions that come from your heart. **Keep the heart pure**.

If you find what you seek, remain vigilant until your departure from this life, and thank God for all His Blessings and Mercy.

SECTION 3
ATTUNEMENT AND INTEGRATION

Each time we commemorate and celebrate the coming of a New Year, groups of entities, separated by geography and beliefs, come together in one way or another to express with hope their desire for change. They may cherish the prospect of a small or large transformation, including that of the most comprehensive change—the advent of the Promised One of God, a Redeemer and Savior, the One who will make things right through Justice and Unity, the One who will bring World Peace.

This scenario, as it repeats itself every year, in different forms of ritualistic expressions and traditions, and through supporters that do not share the same belief system, each with separate expectations since the One acclaimed varies in Name, although of One Source, **tells a tale of our state of consciousness**, the condition we are all in.

Therefore, every time One of the Promised Ones, **These Celestial Beings**, come, **few are the entities that live free from the bondage of**

their space-time conditions and are able ***to recognize*** He Whom God made Manifest for the Day and Age they partake of.

Those entities who ***do not*** recognize that the latest Messenger of God has already come, which entails the great majority, continue to come together and pray, at best hoping for His return. In the worst and more prevalent scenario, entities fight and destroy others who have recognized a Manifestation of God from the past, ***that has a different Name*** from the latest One, though in an absolute sense, all God's Manifestations are One and the same, of the same unimaginable High Station, Emblems of Unity carrying the Holy Spirit to renew the life of every creature in Creation. All the Manifestations express the same Great Spirit with the same Message—we all spring from ***One Source*** and our divine destiny is to live in harmony with each other!

There is only One Creator Who created One Creation, all the creatures of Whom are animated by the same One Breath of Life, One River of God's Love. As this Truth is realized over time, many beings begin to experience the adjustments that integrate and attune their states of conscious-awareness, from one to the next generation, gradually reducing the distortions of their understandings, and increasing their capacities and abilities to recognize and receive the Grace and Blessings from God.

This ***attunement and integration*** has an effect upon the entity's state of conscious-awareness, by integrating and coalescing the ***Soul*** (the engraved Image of God through which He Reveals His Beauty), the ***Spirit*** (as precursor engine and field of imperceptible activities), the ***mind*** (the instrument that allows for thought-forms, comprehension, memory, and vision), and the ***body*** (the unit an entity utilizes to partake in transit and transcendence from one moment to the next—piped, gated, and modulated). During the journey of exploration, discovery, and service to others, this Eternal Soul-possessing Spirit ***remembers and returns*** as an enlightened Self, a member of an eternal civilization experiencing the Reunion with the Beloved.

When this Self unites with an eternal companion in complement (completing always any experience), the two Infinite Spirits experience them-Selves as beings of Light—***<u>enlightened by the Love and Knowledge of the Creator</u>***.

You either see or experience this, or you don't. You are either consciously aware of this, or you are not!

The blessings of God are available to all. The invitation is to search for—and find—the ***golden key***, the ***Word*** of the latest Manifestation, use His Book to open the infinite book of your-Self, and allow the Divine Message for your space-time reality to transform heart and mind....

SECTION 4
COMMUNITIES

As a result of their states of **consciousness** (physiologically-based state of knowing), and **awareness** (Soul-based state of Knowing), entities find themselves responding to **the Call** of the Creator and forming distinct communities as each one advances to be recognized, as proof of his or her own worth and Reality.

In this particular aspect of the journey, we can observe a diverse number of **balloon** (groups of entities) communities, where all sorts of **bubbles** (individual entities) have joined and participate within.

We can identify each balloon community by its intention and attitude, as a collective involved in various reciprocal activities in the theater of life on the planet Earth.

We have affiliations (balloon communities) based on politics, where entities respond to a civic involvement peculiar to their type of governance, script, and role within a structure that can have various forms: tribal, city-state, nationhood, and a world unit-system. These affiliations go further, where the politics involve structural systems beyond any one planetary unified system of intelligent life.

Balloon communities may be based on any interests their members pursue, from sports to scientific inquiry. Entities can belong to one or more balloon communities, and cross into unrelated fields of thought-forms, each with their own unique range and scope, like religious affiliations that separate a world community into systems of unique conscious understandings about one's journey.

These responses to **Calls** from the Creator have **a purpose**. They assist in sieving the many and diverse states of conscious-awareness found amongst His creatures, states that help define and distinguish their ultimate conditions of development, both as individuals and as members of the many balloon communities they have chosen to affiliate themselves with during their journey of **Remembrance and Return, as** they embody the declaration,

"**Here I am My Lord**!"

As each entity advances to be recognized, be called, and be chosen, his journey is a gradual approach towards, or farther away, from God. Each immortal entity can, with each decision, or lack of one, be moving in his or her development ***towards*** a greater understanding of the Whole, or away from God's Will and Desire. In the latter case, he or she is caught in ***a trap and Loop*** of incidents, resulting from following the desires of the ego (the actor or actress), that can go on and on, making each journey a continuum of temporal, fractional existential experiences, until the Light Being is released.

To be chosen and Return represents that moment when an entity joins a community of others that are now experiencing the Eternal. No longer gated in and out of worlds upon worlds that serve a process of development, these Light Beings have been led to the realization of service to Divinity—the end of doubt and the start of certainty! This community lives outside the Realm of journeys.

Beyond the theaters of life, in an existence that brings about perfection, in entities created for that purpose, the enlightened Soul- possessing Spirit joins an eternal civilization made of eternal companions as servants of God. The attunement and integration of the entities' states of conscious-awareness is vital in the process of Remembering and Returning. That is, after responding to ***endless calls of service***, regardless of their type, place, time duration, and other factors, the effects of such laborious involvement ***brings about graduation***—to be chosen!

The many **games and master games** played, consciously or not, are then understood as part of a grand scheme where justice can be observed in the injustice of a moment, where what appears as just was an injustice taking place, where going was returning, and returning was going somewhere else, and where some entities had few choices, while others had many. All of these worlds of contradiction and contrast were lived and experienced **in the name of Self-realization**.

At the end of each temporal, fractional existential experienced, we have either gradually progressed towards that moment when we realize, tenth-dimensionally-speaking, the Oneness and Unity of it All, or we have moved conditionally further away, finding our-Selves far more confused and lost within our ego states (selves)—the actor or actress, **a construct of our vain imaginings**.

SECTION 5
LOVE AND RELATIONS

The Love of God is the motive power in Creation. It is the reason behind it. To be consciously aware of God's Love is to Know about Eternal Life.

The way the authors have experienced the Love of God, in a personal sense, is by practicing what could be called **sensual chasteness**. In this way of intimate sharing, the couple enjoys sensual bliss of a higher dimensional order by using the senses in a refined and subtle way, particularly the sense of touch. This refinement occurs as a result of opening up to the Divine Modulation and gift of God's Love, as the couple hugs, kisses, and caresses one another. By surrendering to the Divine Love reflected by their eternal companionship, each one becomes not only closer to God, but also to the beloved companion.

After all, what could be more eternal than the Love of God? In fact, logically speaking, why would anyone want to put all the effort it takes to sustain a relationship, without the assurance that such a relationship should last eternally? God does not want His people to waste time, surely.

What conditions must be fulfilled for a married couple to love one another with this higher level of light, bliss, and delight?

Since God is transcendent, beyond His creation, and the Creator is only accessible through His Manifestations, who carry His presence through the Holy Spirit to Earth—within Their Embodiments and Words—recognition of He Whom God made Manifest is paramount.

Once the eternal companions have achieved this acknowledgement, they are in alignment to receive the correct flow and frequency of Love for their time-space continuum. Like two tiny drops of water in a clear mountain stream, they are swept to the Sea of Infinite Awareness together, basking in the noon Sunlight of infinite Love.

Is there a sacrifice required? Of course. How else would God know that we are serious, that we love God above all things?

Women on Earth, by the nature of things in their journey at the present time, by birthing, nurturing, and caring for the children, their families and larger communities, are, in general, already sacrificing. This sacrifice is known to God.

Men, here, are required to be strong, courageous, and detached from the animal passions which lower their consciousness and awareness, to avoid sexual intercourse unless the couple has agreed, after much prayer and consultation, to be the care-givers of a new comer who will make mention of God.

What is the reward for the couple who practices God-given Love? By not focusing on a six-second orgasm, and that which addicts him to that third-dimensional sensation, such as pornography or other practices, he can release the false impression that women are objects to be used and discarded. The man now focuses on the woman with his Sun-like energy from his Light Being. She in turn, receives his Light, like a tree blossoming in Spring, enlivening and nourishing her Spirit and Soul. Basking in the radiance of Love gifted from the Omnipotent One, the man and woman are both able to experience hours of bliss, a bliss that will continue throughout the Day of God in the Garden of Eternity.

Section 6

In Closing

A quick summary may help ***you understand*** the need to integrate your Soul-based state of awareness with your physiologically-based state of consciousness during this fractional and temporal existential (human) experience—it may have been called something else elsewhere.

This is a door, an opportunity to go through and be transformed. The authors have previously presented a narrative (see <u>Echoes of a Vision of... Paradise: If You Cannot Remember, You Will Return</u>), Volumes 1, 2 and 3, that puts together a case for you to comprehend how easily it is to be erroneously programmed into accepting and living any life-style. Some of these ways of living are promoted by society itself, while others are abhorred and outright rejected in principle, or condemned through laws.

No matter what the life-style is, or how immoral or unethical the societal practice is, it may have been accepted by the community for quite some time, even practiced over several generations until, mysteriously or not, it finds its way out of society's favor—the institution of slavery, for example!

It is so easy to see how social and individual consciousness are influenced by personal desire and limited by competitive outlooks in the arena of life. When we contemplate how varied the social field of activities has been throughout history, we cannot fail to realize that our direction as a social order was, and is, the result of those in power. It is they whose dictates eventually take us all down the pathway of war and self-destruction, annihilating in their wake the environment and other living organisms sharing a world that is no longer viable as is, or livable collectively.

We go through wars like any other activity, until they end because they have to end—then, the remaining living simply have to clean up the mess. We rehash the past to derive some sense from it, supposedly to avert the same catastrophe again. Looking back never works because we are trapped in the same state of consciousness!

And so, the merry-go-around of activities continues, with some changes of course.

Once in a while, an infusion of Divinely-ordained energies transforms the capacity of the entities arriving to inhabit a planet, a Dispensation meant to affect the mind and the heart of an ongoing civilization struggling to consciously advance and survive.

However, few are the ones able to graduate from a preceding cycle, and many are the ones that remain and fall behind. A tug of war ensues between those that pursue Unity as a means to an end, and those that see unity as an obstacle to their selfish ways.

Activities of the latter individuals and communities promote separation and disturbance, instead of bringing us all closer together in our relationships, leading eventually to a rise in the levels of conflict and tragedy, time and again. The light of change and hope is lost through the fog of dismay and suffering, and a race of entities meant to **Remember and Return** find them-Selves caught in the quagmire of a collective delusion and denial once more, despite the fact that the Manifestation of God, once again, has brought them *the Elixir that transforms the heart*, allowing Soul and Spirit to return to the Pavilion of His Glory.

When the heart is transformed in this way, the inner senses respond to a range of previously unknown activities, bringing information that fulfills the needs and requirements of a third-dimensional moment with solutions that would otherwise remain limited with our third- and fourth-dimensional states of consciousness. Our Divine Nature is now active, providing the impetus impelling collaboration with the Divine Plan, a Plan previously unknown—we are aware that we are aware!

There is nothing more satisfactory than to walk the path of our journey Knowing why we are here, what our purpose is, and with whom we are to travel forever—the eternal companion of each divinely- ordained partnership, with whom we experience the blessings and understandings gifted to us as we both are transformed into that image which more and more closely reveals the Beauty of God, our Creator.

Every entity in Creation is invited to remember and return to the Creator of All. It is up to each of us not to barter His desires for ours, with our temporal and fractional wishing adorning our incomplete understanding. Not Knowing the endless Divine Gifts of which we are invited to partake, we require, at first, an act of faith, to be patient and forgo selfish pleasures for those bounties God will bestow when He deems we are ready. It behooves us to throw our lot on the side of the Great Mystery, when faced with a world as distorted as ours, a world whose condition tells us clearly that there must be something we are missing from within—yet to be discovered.

The main objective of searching for **Paradise** is to approach the Creator and place a signal within the heart that says,

I am ready to Love Thee without resisting Thy Will and Desire for us all—we must love God first, for His Love to reach us!

What you observe and understand is where you are conditionally in a state of consciousness—in a life pre-ordained to bring you any and all necessary experiences required for your development. You are tested, challenged and gradually assessed by the unified system of intelligent life that anticipates every thought-form and action to be taken, seamlessly, without disruptions that would give away the continuous flow that gives the appearances of cause and effect in space and over time.

You are in a loop that repeats itself, enmeshed in events that can keep you in a journey that knows no end until charged with the necessary energies (information that comes from without) catapulting you into another orb of understanding. Trapped in a mind-world construct of your own making, you do not know why life is the way it is—whether you are rich and famous this time around, or in a life of abject poverty. Whatever possible outcome we can imagine—hell or heaven are appearances in a world of vain imaginings—each life is purposefully designed to invite each entity to approach the Creator and begin the journey of remembrance and return. Not until this invitation is accepted will the true journey begin.

ACKNOWLEDGMENTS

In light of the enormity of information that has contributed to weave the texture of this narrative, we first acknowledge *every Manifestation of God* whose transit and transcendence through this temporal and fractional existential experience has influenced and continues to influence, the many communities of the *Called* answering to the *Clarion Call of the Beloved*.

There are also a diverse number of faithful and fruitful Light Beings that have come and gone throughout the ages, whose depository of knowledge and whose lives have, in one way or another, contributed to the advancement of civilization.

Deserving a mention as well are the numerous entities that, though unnamed, have contributed, and continue to contribute, from moment-to-moment, to the well-being of others. In this respect, there are those that have expanded the understanding of our local unified system of intelligent life, having the temerity to present ideas that were and are meant to push the envelope of human understanding in a unifying direction, despite the resistance or interference from others.

There is, finally, a fifth-dimensional flow of packets of information whose source and origin can be considered divine, from those whose ascendency as Light Beings adorn the firmament of possible outcomes—since service is an eternal mandate!

About the Authors

Frank Scott and Nisa Montie joined forces to aid the enlightenment of humanity. Since his youth, Frank has been gifted with unusual experiences that inform and provide a map that helps direct each entity on the divine path of truth. Nisa uses animal and fairy characters to teach virtues in joy-filled children's tales.

Printed in the United States
By Bookmasters